# Memo Devo

## Memorization as Devotion

"Sanctify them in the Truth. Your Word is Truth."
John 17:17

Steve Cook

Memo Devo: Memorization as Devotion

Published by Five Talents Audio
Copyright 2014 by Five Talents Audio
ISBN#: 978-0-9821616-7-8

Printed in the USA

For more information:
Five Talents Audio
770-518-8336

# Memo Devo (Memorization as Devotion)
## Introduction

Welcome to a whole new, yet extremely ancient, method of Bible study.

In August of 2009, I was where a lot of long-time Christians end up. I was quite dissatisfied with my relationship with Jesus. Whenever I did think about Him outside of church, which was rare, I felt I had little intimacy with Him. Plus, I had always had a timidity in my witness for Him that wasn't getting any better. And perhaps worst of all, I felt like I rarely gained any real victories in my recurring struggles against the enemy personally.

Now, I'm a professional actor, and coincidentally at that same time I had started memorizing long passages of Scripture for dramatic presentations. And all I can tell you is that from that time until now, my relationship with Jesus has never grown so deep, so fast. I have never felt more intimate, confident, protected and, most importantly, more IN LOVE with Jesus.

It's as if my heart has been awakened, not only to new truths in Scripture, but also to a deep thirst for more of them. I wake up every day as if I have found a new "workout" that's guaranteed to bring the result I desire: namely, to bring my will more in line with Jesus' will. And all I have to do is commit to doing one simple exercise every day – letting Jesus' words literally ABIDE in me, as He encourages me to do in John 15:7-8.

I know. It sounds too simple, right? Too remedial. Memorization is the "lowest form of learning" right? Well, maybe, maybe not. But think about it this way. For almost half of our recorded existence (2700 years), God chose NOT to have His Word written down at all. And even after that it wasn't widely distributed in written form for thousands more years, certainly when Jesus taught. If you don't believe that, just check out the Beth Sefers of His day or how many times He starts a teaching in the Sermon on the Mount with "You have heard it said..." rather than "You have read..." when referring to Scripture. People HAD to memorize God's Word through story and song if they were going to share it, and then trust the Holy Spirit to sanctify them through that process.

And that is finally what Memo Devo is: the literal ingesting of God's Word into my body, with the intention of speaking it back to someone else and then letting the Spirit do His promised work of sanctification in both of us. Period.

I chose these 8 passages only as a starting place, because I believe they hold truths that are essential to anyone's healthy and growing walk with Jesus. They have been assembled by length order, but feel free to skip around as the Spirit leads.

Within each devotion are a couple of suggestions for how to memorize each day's verse(s), using simple mnemonics and something I like to call the "Tide Technique". It is the same technique and tools that I use when putting together my own live Scripture presentations. You can learn more about that on my website at www.5talentsaudio.com. Trust me, I try to make this as fun and easy for myself as possible. #:-D

One final caveat though, **make sure you don't skip the final step of actually SPEAKING BACK the entire passage to someone else.** This is sooo important and without question the real difference-maker in this process. I don't go back and recite everything, every day, usually just the verse for that day and then the whole thing on Friday or the weekend. It provides not only an accountability element, but also opportunities for the Spirit to sanctify others in the Truth. Believe me, He does, and it is so exciting... especially when He does it in my kids! It is similar to Charlotte Mason's "narration" philosophy. The one major difference to me is that the Bible, unlike any other 'living' book, was written by God and therefore having its specific words literally abide in me is very important because they have the unique power of sanctification. (John 17:17)

So that's it. I'm so glad you've decided to give Memo Devo a shot with me! I have to tell you, I am almost envious of the experience you are about to have because I really do believe that after trying it for a month or two, you will experience the same results that I have. That is, that the Holy Spirit will begin to move in your life like never before, and you will have better intimacy with God, a better witness for God and better protection under the wings of God than you have ever experienced before. How exciting!

And that's Jesus' promise, not mine. Well, ok mine too.

Blessings Today,
Steve Cook

# Memo Devo

8 Devotionals
Designed to Help You Start
Hiding More Scripture in Your Heart

"If you abide in Me, and My words abide in you, you shall ask what
you will and it shall be given you. This is to My Father's glory, that
you bear much fruit, showing yourselves to be my disciples."
John 15:7-8

1) **Isaiah 55:8-11** (The Power of the Word)
2) **Titus 3:3-7** (The Gospel)
3) **2Corinthians 11:2-6** (No Other Gospel)
4) **1John 4:20-5:3** (Cultural Challenges)
5) **Psalm 78:2-7** (Family Discipleship)
6) **1Corinthians 13:1-10** (Love)
7) **Matthew 5:3-16** (The Beatitudes)
8) **John 1:1-18** (Jesus' Deity, Our Adoption)

# "The Power of the Word"
## Isaiah 55:8-11

# Memo Devo
## Isaiah 55:8-11
## Subject: The Power of the Word

**DAYS 1 & 2**
**Isaiah 55:8-9**

8 For my <u>thoughts</u> are not your <u>thoughts</u>. Neither are your <u>ways</u> my <u>ways</u>, says the Lord.
9 For as the <u>heavens</u> are <u>higher</u> than the earth, so are my <u>ways</u> higher than your <u>ways</u>, and my <u>thoughts</u> above your <u>thoughts</u>.

**Mnemonic: "TWA"**

I bite off two verses today and give myself an extra day or two to get them down. I do this because there's a great mnemonic that works for these first two verses together, "TWA". All I do is remember that well-known acronym both forward and backward to come up with the underlined keywords above. T-W-A-W-T.

I know, I know, since when do 'heavens' and 'higher' start with 'A', right? Well, bear with me a bit. When pronounced, the letter 'H' does begin with an 'A' and actually sounds like an 'A' until the very last second, sooo...:-P. Hey, with my brain, anything goes sometimes (as I'm sure will be true of yours also) and this does actually work for me. In truth, I have found that the odder the better when it comes to memory aids. As long as it's not too far out. So be creative! You'll know the difference.

From there it's an easy walk through these first two verses. Then, once I am able to say the two verses without looking at them, it's time for me to begin putting them in my short-term memory. And there's no better way to do that than sheer repetition. This is just hard work, I'll be honest. But I've also grown accustomed to the Spirit honoring this work with many subtle and overt revelations during this time. A good rule of thumb for hiding a verse deep in your short-term memory is at least 10 repetitions per verse on the first pass.

Memo Devo
**Isaiah 55:8-11**
**Subject: The Power of the Word**

**DAY 3**
**Isaiah 55:10**

10 Surely as the <u>rain</u> and <u>snow</u> come down from heaven and do not <u>return</u> there but <u>water</u> the earth, making it bring forth and <u>bud</u>, giving s<u>eed</u> to the sower and <u>bread</u> to the eater,

**Point to Ponder**

I find this verse and the next one to be two of the most flowing and poetic verses in the entire Bible, requiring less practical assistance to memorize them. They're just that beautiful. However, I continue to underline keywords, even though I have no mnemonic in place. This helps me group phrases together in my mind, using a single word trigger. It works similar to a phenomenon known as "typoglycemia" whereby our brains are able to complete words even if we only have the first and last letters in the proper place. Tihs is bcuseae the huamn mnid deos not raed ervey lteter by istlef. Nor do we read, at least in my experience, every word by itself either.

**The Tide Technique**

After having put verse 10 in my short-term memory, rather than going back to verse 8 and trying to run all three verses that I have learned together just yet, I first only go back to verse 9 and begin there, running 9 and 10 until I can do just those two comfortably. Only then do I go back and add verse 8 and try to do the whole thing together, like a tide slowly going in and out over the whole passage until it's solidified in my long-term memory and ready for testing. This process is really cool because even though I am actually repeating the verses more often than if I were doing a traditional approach of going back to the beginning every time, my brain feels less stressed and is more encouraged by more successful run-throughs of smaller sections.

Memo Devo
**Isaiah 55:8-11**
**Subject: The Power of the Word**

**DAY 4**
**Isaiah 55:11**

11 So <u>shall</u> my Word be that <u>goes</u> out of My mouth. It shall not <u>return</u> to Me void, but shall <u>accomplish</u> that which I will. And it shall <u>prosper</u> in the thing whereto I sent it.

I always have extra anticipation when a famous verse is included in the long passage I'm memorizing. I know it's going to help me ground that truth in the context God intends, which is almost always a different context than the one I had before.

**Put It Together Using the *Tide Technique**

8 For my <u>thoughts</u> are not your <u>thoughts</u>. Neither are your <u>ways</u> my <u>ways</u>, says the Lord.
9 For as the <u>heavens</u> are <u>higher</u> than the earth, so are my <u>ways</u> higher than your <u>ways</u>, and my <u>thoughts</u> above your <u>thoughts</u>.
10 Surely as the <u>rain</u> and <u>snow</u> come down from heaven and do not <u>return</u> there but <u>water</u> the earth, making it bring forth and <u>bud</u>, giving <u>seed</u> to the sower and <u>bread</u> to the eater,
11 So <u>shall</u> my Word be that <u>goes</u> out of My mouth. It shall not <u>return</u> to Me void, but shall <u>accomplish</u> that which I will. And it shall <u>prosper</u> in the thing whereto I sent it.

*More information on the Tide Technique can be found elsewhere in this book and also on my instructional video "Bible Play: The Value of Dramatization in Memorization" available at 5talentsaudio.com.

# "The Gospel"
## Titus 3:3-7

Memo Devo
**Titus 3:3-7**
**Subject: The Gospel**

**DAY 1**
**Titus 3:3**

3 For we <u>ourselves</u> also were in times <u>past</u> <u>unwise</u>, <u>disobedient</u>, <u>deceived</u>, serving the <u>lusts</u> and diverse <u>pleasures</u>, living in <u>maliciousness</u> and <u>envy</u>, <u>hateful</u>, and <u>hating</u> one another.

**Mnemonic: "PUDDLe ME in Hate"**

I love this verse's detailed description of exactly why EVERYONE needs Jesus so desperately. It uses slightly different keywords in different translations, but in the 1599 Geneva Bible, which I use, this mnemonic helps me to recall them more easily. I especially anchor to the ME in the middle because it is so logical for the keywords it represents.

In August of 2009, when I first began memorizing and dramatizing long passages of Scripture, I also began to petition the Holy Spirit for new and more effective ways to approach the lost. I had come to realize that there is often a kind of "Gospel fatigue" among unbelievers with single verses like John 3:16 and 8:32. People sometimes tune them out as soon as they are brought up because they are so familiar. Not that these single verses have no power of course. They are as powerful as the Spirit would like in any situation. But in terms of how my message was being received, I began to feel God was giving me this passage as an alternative "elevator Gospel" if you will. One that could still be quoted quickly, but goes a little deeper and is more likely not to have been heard before by an unbeliever. It also really shows my own depravity right away and lets someone know that I am "living in sin" and in need of a savior just as much as they are. The only difference is that I know it.

Memo Devo
**Titus 3:3-7**
**Subject: The Gospel**

**DAYS 2-4**
**Titus 3:4-6**

4 But when that <u>bountifulness</u> and that <u>love</u> of God our <u>Savior</u> toward man <u>appeared</u>, 5 <u>not</u> by the works of <u>righteousness</u>, which <u>we</u> had done, but according to His <u>mercy</u> He saved us, by the <u>washing</u> of the new birth, and the <u>renewing</u> of the Holy Ghost, 6 which He <u>shed</u> on us <u>abundantly</u>, through <u>Jesus</u> Christ our <u>Savior</u>,

A big chunk here, but it's easier to memorize than taking each verse separately because it is three parts of a single thought. No mnemonics jump out here either unfortunately, but if I concentrate on those underlined keywords, I can at least isolate the main thoughts: "But then God's love appeared, not because of me, but because of Him, and washed me clean like new with the Spirit of Jesus." I'd give myself a few days on this section alone.

### Put It Together Using the *Tide Technique

3 For we <u>ourselves </u>also were in times <u>past</u> <u>unwise</u>, <u>disobedient</u>, <u>deceived</u>, serving the <u>lusts</u> and diverse pleasures, living in <u>maliciousness</u> and <u>envy</u>, <u>hateful</u>, and <u>hating</u> one another.
4 But when that <u>bountifulness</u> and that <u>love</u> of God our <u>Savior</u> toward man <u>appeared</u>, 5 <u>not</u> by the works of <u>righteousness</u>, which <u>we</u> had done, but according to His <u>mercy</u> He saved us, by the <u>washing</u> of the new birth, and the <u>renewing</u> of the Holy Ghost, 6 which He <u>shed</u> on us <u>abundantly</u>, through <u>Jesus</u> Christ our <u>Savior</u>,

*Remember, start at the end and "tide" your way back slowly.

Memo Devo
**Titus 3:3-7**
**Subject: The Gospel**

**DAY 5**
**Titus 3:7**

7 That we, being <u>justified</u> by His <u>grace</u>, should be made <u>heirs</u> according to the <u>hope</u> of eternal life.

This verse, like John 3:16, is only a partial statement of the Gospel in that it only concentrates on what God did for us, not why He had to do it. People have a hard time grasping that there literally are no "good" people on this earth as far as God is concerned (Mk10:18). We either don't believe it or we just plain refuse to consider the possibility that without the free gift of God's grace, we DESERVE the eternal torment of His wrath. And that goes for a lot of us Christians too! We need to make sure those who would hear our message understand first how desperately we all need to repent before we can truly grab hold of God's mercy and grace. This passage does that very well.

**Put It Together Using the Tide Technique**

3 For we <u>ourselves </u>also were in times <u>past</u> <u>unwise</u>, <u>disobedient</u>, <u>deceived</u>, serving the <u>lusts</u> and diverse pleasures, living in <u>maliciousness</u> and <u>envy</u>, <u>hateful</u>, and <u>hating </u>one another.
4 But when that <u>bountifulness</u> and that <u>love</u> of God our <u>Savior</u> toward man <u>appeared</u>, 5 <u>not</u> by the works of <u>righteousness</u>, which <u>we</u> had done, but according to His <u>mercy</u> He saved us, by the <u>washing</u> of the new birth, and the <u>renewing</u>
of the Holy Ghost, 6 which He <u>shed</u> on us <u>abundantly</u>, through <u>Jesus</u> Christ our <u>Savior</u>,
7 That we, being <u>justified</u> by His <u>grace</u>, should be made <u>heirs</u> according to the <u>hope</u> of eternal life.

# "No Other Gospel"

## 2Corinthians 11:2-6

Memo Devo
**2Corinthians 11:2-6**
**Subject: No Other Gospel** (Mormonism, JW, etc.)

**DAY 1**
**2Corinthians 11:2**

2 For I am <u>jealous</u> over you, with a <u>godly</u> jealousy. For I have <u>prepared</u> you for one <u>husband</u>, to <u>present</u> you as a pure <u>virgin</u> to Christ.

**Mnemonic: "Prepared to Present as Pure"**

I find this passage to be a great conversation starter with both invited and uninvited guests at my door (if you know what I mean, :P) "What if Paul were here with us right now? What do you think he would say about extra-biblical faiths in light if these words he has written?"

Otherwise, the imagery of this opening statement about following false gospels is quite clear and logical, so not much is needed to trigger the sequence of keywords once they are in my short-term memory. In cases like this, all I try to do is picture those keywords first and then try to fill in the phrases around them. Once I have done that, I just keep repeating it until I'm comfortable.

**Point to Ponder**

Paul is speaking to "the bride of Christ", or the church at Corinth. I find it interesting that just as in Genesis 2:24 , the marriage at the end of the age will be the same as it was in the beginning, between one bride and one Husband.

Memo Devo
**2Corinthians 11:2-6**
**Subject: No Other Gospel** (Mormonism, JW, etc.)

**DAY 2**
**2Corinthians 11:3**

3 For I <u>fear</u> that <u>as</u> the <u>serpent</u> <u>tricked</u> <u>Eve</u> with his subtlety, so your <u>minds</u> may be <u>corrupted</u> from the <u>simplicity</u> that is in Christ.

**Mnemonic: "FAST Evey MCSimple"**

Hey don't laugh, it works for me! The caps correspond to the underlined keywords. I love these kinds of mnemonics because they are obviously fun, but also because they are exactly what I think a good mnemonic should be: odd enough to stand out from everyday language but not too way out to be ineffective. For example: the mnemonic "OGOSHMUSIC" triggers a keyword in each of the 10 Commandments for me. As a result, I will forever be able to remember all 10 in order immediately. Ask me how effective that tool is in daily life situations with my kids or when witnessing God's love to others?

**\*Put It Together**

2 For I am <u>jealous</u> over you, with a <u>godly</u> jealousy. For I have <u>prepared</u> you for one <u>husband</u>, to <u>present</u> you as a pure <u>virgin</u> to Christ.
3 For I <u>fear</u> that <u>as</u> the <u>serpent</u> <u>tricked</u> <u>Eve</u> with his subtlety, so your <u>minds</u> may be <u>corrupted</u> from the <u>simplicity</u> that is in Christ.

\*I find a good rule of thumb during this first short-term memorization stage is 10 repetitions. And don't forget to speak it back to someone else! #:-D Get more tips at 5talentsaudio.com

Memo Devo
**2Corinthians 11:2-6**
**Subject: No Other Gospel** (Mormonism, JW, etc.)

**DAY 3**
**2Corinthians 11:4**

4 That is, if someone comes to you <u>preaching</u> a <u>Jesus</u> whom we have not preached, or you receive a <u>spirit</u> or a <u>gospel</u> which you have not <u>received</u>, you might well put up with him.

**Mnemonic: "PJs SuGaR"**

And the silly hits just keep on comin'! Obviously another fun one. But believe it or not, this actually helps my brain not only reference the keywords in the verse but also puts them in their proper and logical context, allowing the Spirit to work as I recite them.

**The Tide Technique**

After having put verse 4 in my short-term memory, rather than going back to verse 2 and trying to run all three verses together just yet, I first only go back to verse 3 and begin there, running 3 and 4 until I can do just those without looking. Only then do I go back and add verse 2 and try to do the whole passage together, like a tide slowly going in and out over the whole passage until it's solidified in my long-term memory and ready for testing. Although I've never done a "scientific" comparison, I really do feel I am repeating the verses more often this way than if I were doing a traditional approach of going back to the beginning every time. And I think it's mostly because my brain feels less fatigued and is more encouraged by more successful run-throughs of smaller sections.

Memo Devo
**2Corinthians 11:2-6**
**Subject: No Other Gospel** (Mormonism, JW, etc.)

**DAYS 4&5**
**2Corinthians 11:5-6**

5 For surely I am <u>not</u> <u>inferior</u> to even the very <u>chief</u> of these "Apostles".
6 For though I am unskilled in speaking, I am not so in knowledge, and <u>among</u> you we have made ourselves <u>clearly</u> <u>understood</u> in all <u>things</u>.

### Mnemonic: "NICe And CUTe"

Two more silly hits for the road! I put these last two verses together over two days mostly because for me it's easier to remember the words "NICe And CUTe" together than separately. I realize it leaves out several keywords, but try it. Again, as I repeat the verses, my brain immediately begins to finish out the phrases logically as I begin to anchor to even just a few keywords. It's really amazing to me!

### Put It Together Using the Tide Technique

2 For I am <u>jealous</u> over you, with a <u>godly</u> jealousy. For I have <u>prepared</u> you for one <u>husband</u>, to <u>present</u> you as a pure <u>virgin</u> to Christ.
3 For I <u>fear</u> that <u>as</u> the <u>serpent</u> <u>tricked</u> <u>Eve</u> with his subtlety, so your <u>minds</u> may be <u>corrupted</u> from the <u>simplicity</u> that is in Christ.
4 That is, if someone comes to you <u>preaching</u> a <u>Jesus</u> whom we have not preached, or you receive a <u>spirit</u> or a <u>gospel</u> which you have not <u>received</u>, you might well put up with him.
5 For surely I am <u>not</u> <u>inferior</u> to even the very <u>chief</u> of these "Apostles".
6 For though I am unskilled in speaking, I am not so in knowledge, and <u>among</u> you we have made ourselves <u>clearly</u> <u>understood</u> in all <u>things</u>.

# "Cultural Challenges"
## 1John 4:20-5:3

Memo Devo
**1John 4:20-5:3**
**Subject: Cultural Challenges** (abortion, sexuality, etc...)

**DAY 1**
**1John 4:20**

20 <u>Whoever</u> says he <u>loves</u> God, but <u>hates</u> his <u>brother</u>, he is a <u>liar</u>. For <u>how</u> can one who does <u>not</u> <u>love</u> his <u>brother</u>, whom he has <u>seen</u>, <u>love God</u>, whom he has <u>not seen</u>?

**Mnemonic: "Your Lyin' Eyes"**

Not really a mnemonic in the classic sense, but it does state exactly what this verse is all about. The simplicity is so logical and convicting, it's just a matter of practicing how John says it. A minimum of 10 repetitions is a good benchmark for this early short-term memorization stage.

**Point to Ponder**

This is the first reference verse for much of the liberal theology agenda today. However, once I ponder the whole long passage, I get the whole context of what God is saying in this verse. Love for my brother is but the first half of the equation. Repentance and love for God is the other and more important half. (Mark 12:30)

Memo Devo
**1John 4:20-5:3**
**Subject: Cultural Challenges** (abortion, sexuality, etc...)


**DAY 2**
**1John 4:21**


21 And this <u>commandment</u> we have from Him, "He who loves <u>God</u>, should also love his <u>brother</u>."


John says essentially, "Hey, if you don't believe me, believe Jesus' 2<sup>nd</sup> Commandment, 'Love your neighbor as yourself.'" (Mark 12:31)


**\*Put It Together**

20 <u>Whoever</u> says he <u>loves</u> God, but <u>hates</u> his <u>brother</u>, he is a <u>liar</u>. For <u>how</u> can one who does <u>not</u> <u>love</u> his <u>brother</u>, whom he has <u>seen</u>, <u>love God</u>, whom he has <u>not seen</u>?
21 And this <u>commandment</u> we have from Him, "He who loves God, should also love his brother."


\*Again, a good rule of thumb during this first short-term memorization stage is 10 repetitions. Then it's really best to go ahead and recite each verse each day for someone else. But if I can't do that, a fun way to check if something is getting into my long-term memory is to speak the verse back out loud to myself while juggling or folding laundry or doing some other simple task that creates a mild distraction for my brain. Some days are tougher than others! I try VERY HARD to stay on schedule, but I will give myself an extra day to repeat the same devo if things come up or I just don't feel ready to move on.

Memo Devo
**1John 4:20-5:3**
**Subject: Cultural Challenges** (abortion, sexuality, etc...)

**DAY 3**
**1John 5:1**

1 <u>Whoever</u> <u>believes</u> that Jesus is the <u>Christ</u>, has been <u>born</u> of God. And whoever <u>loves</u> <u>God</u>, loves <u>those</u> who have been <u>born</u> of <u>Him</u>.

**Mnemonic: none**

Anyone who has genuinely repented of their sin and trusts Jesus as their only Way back to the Father is my brother or sister. From Messianic Jews to former jihadists to past LGBT Presidents. As such, they are not only deserving of my joyous love and forgiveness as children of God, they should expect it. Period. As for those unrepentant, well Jesus says that's where He comes in. (Matthew 5:43-48, Mark 10: 26-31)

**Put It Together Using the *Tide Technique**

20 <u>Whoever</u> says he <u>loves</u> God, but <u>hates</u> his <u>brother</u>, he is a <u>liar</u>. For <u>how </u>can one who does <u>not</u> <u>love</u> his <u>brother</u>, whom he has <u>seen</u>, <u>love God</u>, whom he has <u>not seen</u>?
21 And this <u>commandment</u> we have from Him, "He who loves God, should also love his brother."
5:1 <u>Whoever</u> <u>believes</u> that Jesus is the <u>Christ</u>, has been <u>born</u> of God. And whoever <u>loves</u> <u>God</u>, loves <u>those</u> who have been <u>born</u> of <u>Him</u>.

*More information on the Tide Technique can also be found on my instructional video "Bible Play: The Value of Dramatization in Memorization" at 5talentsaudio.com.

Memo Devo
**1John 4:20-5:3**
**Subject: Cultural Challenges** (abortion, sexuality, etc...)

**DAY 4**
**1John 5:2**

2 And this is <u>how</u> we <u>know</u> that we <u>love</u> the <u>children</u> of God; when we <u>love God</u> and <u>keep</u> His <u>commandments</u>.

**Mnemonic: none**

Another explicit statement of the order of the 1<sup>st</sup> and 2<sup>nd</sup> Commandments given by Jesus. They are not interchangeable. The prerequisite to loving my neighbor is loving God. And Jesus says the best way to do that is by obeying His commandments. (John 14:15)

**Put It Together Using the Tide Technique**

20 <u>Whoever</u> says he <u>loves</u> God, but <u>hates</u> his <u>brother</u>, he is a liar. For <u>how</u> can one who does <u>not</u> <u>love</u> his <u>brother</u>, whom he has <u>seen</u>, <u>love God</u>, whom he has <u>not seen</u>?
21 And this <u>commandment</u> we have from Him, "He who loves God, should also love his brother."
5:1 <u>Whoever</u> <u>believes</u> that Jesus is the <u>Christ</u>, has been <u>born</u> of God. And whoever <u>loves</u> <u>God</u>, loves <u>those</u> who have been <u>born</u> of <u>Him</u>.
2 And this is <u>how</u> we <u>know</u> that we <u>love</u> the <u>children</u> of God; when we <u>love God</u> and <u>keep</u> His <u>commandments</u>.

Memo Devo
**1John 4:20-5:3**
**Subject: Cultural Challenges** (abortion, sexuality, etc...)

**DAY 5**
**1John 5:3**

3 For this <u>is</u> the <u>love</u> of God, when we <u>keep</u> His <u>commandments</u>. And His commandments are not <u>burdensome</u>.

In case there was any doubt about the best way to show my love for God, as is so often done in the Bible, John says it twice here. But importantly I think, he then is quick to point out that doing so is not a hardship. In fact, as Jesus says in John 15:7, the more I love God by having His words abide in me, the more I receive, because the more my will begins to conform to His will.

**Put It Together Using the Tide Technique**

20 <u>Whoever</u> says he <u>loves</u> God, but <u>hates</u> his <u>brother</u>, he is a <u>liar</u>. For <u>how</u> can one who does <u>not</u> <u>love</u> his <u>brother</u>, whom he has <u>seen</u>, <u>love God</u>, whom he has <u>not seen</u>?
21 And this <u>commandment</u> we have from Him, "He who loves God, should also love his brother."
5:1 <u>Whoever</u> <u>believes</u> that Jesus is the <u>Christ</u>, has been <u>born</u> of God. And whoever <u>loves</u> <u>God</u>, loves <u>those</u> who have been <u>born</u> of <u>Him</u>.
2 And this is <u>how</u> we <u>know</u> that we <u>love</u> the <u>children</u> of God; when we <u>love God</u> and <u>keep</u> His <u>commandments</u>.
3 For this <u>is</u> the <u>love</u> of God, when we <u>keep</u> His <u>commandments</u>. And His commandments are not <u>burdensome</u>.

# "Family Discipleship"
## Psalm 78:2-7

Memo Devo
**Psalm 78:2-7**
**Subject: Family Discipleship**

**DAY 1**
**Psalm 78:2**

2 I will open my <u>mouth</u> in a <u>parable</u>. I will <u>declare</u> the high <u>sentences</u> of old.

This is the 1599 Geneva Bible translation. I love the way it states the second sentence. Many translations use the phrase "dark sayings" of old. The Hebrew word is "chidyah" which means "riddle" or "enigma" and in this context, I think "high sentences" is not only a more poetic translation, but also more accurate.

**Point to Ponder**

In my opinion, Psalm 78:2-7 is the Bible's strongest call to family discipleship (especially to us Dads) by way of long-passage memorization. It is the Mission Passage of my ministry, Five Talents Audio.

Memo Devo
**Psalm 78:2-7**
**Subject: Family Discipleship**

**DAY 2**
**Psalm 78:3**

3 Which we have <u>heard</u> and <u>known</u>, and our <u>fathers</u> have <u>told</u> us.

This verse makes no mistake as to who is to assume the leadership role in the passing on of God's truth to the next generation: that is, us fathers.

**\*Put It Together**

2 I will open my <u>mouth</u> in a <u>parable</u>. I will <u>declare</u> the high <u>sentences</u> of old.
3 Which we have <u>heard</u> and <u>known</u>, and our <u>fathers</u> have <u>told</u> us.

\*I find a good rule of thumb during this first short-term memorization stage is 10 repetitions. Then it's really best to go ahead and recite each verse each day for someone else. But if I can't do that, a fun way to check if something is getting into my long-term memory is to speak the verse back out loud to myself while juggling or folding laundry or doing some other simple task that creates a mild distraction for my brain. Some days are tougher than others! I try VERY HARD to stay on schedule, but I will give myself an extra day to repeat the same devo if things come up or I just don't feel ready to move on.

Memo Devo
**Psalm 78:2-7**
**Subject: Family Discipleship**

**DAY 3**
**Psalm 78:4**

4 We will not <u>hide</u> them from their <u>children</u>. But to the <u>generation</u> that is to come, we will show the <u>praise</u> of the Lord, His <u>power</u> also, and His <u>wonderful</u> <u>works</u> that He has done.


**Mnemonic: "Double PW"**

This verse, although a bit long, is a logical completion to the previous verse. That always helps a LOT. It's still talking about the "high sentences of old", but it begins with what I pledge NOT to do: hide them. Then it quickly moves to the specific things I WILL do instead, and for that I have the simple little rhythmic mnemonic: "Double PW" for "praise", "power", "wonderful" and "works".

**Put It Together Using the *Tide Technique**

2 I will open my <u>mouth</u> in a parable. I will <u>declare</u> the high <u>sentences</u> of old.
3 Which we have <u>heard</u> and <u>known</u>, and our <u>fathers</u> have <u>told</u> us.
4 We will not <u>hide</u> them from their <u>children</u>. But to the <u>generation</u> that is to come, we will show the <u>praise</u> of the Lord, His <u>power</u> also, and His <u>wonderful</u> <u>works</u> that He has done.


*More information on the Tide Technique can be found elsewhere in this book and also on my instructional video "Bible Play: The Value of Dramatization in Memorization" available at 5talentsaudio.com.

Memo Devo
**Psalm 78:2-7**
**Subject: Family Discipleship**

**DAY 4**
**Psalm 78:5**

5 How He established a <u>testimony</u> in <u>Jacob</u>, and ordained a <u>Law</u> in <u>Israel</u>, which He <u>commanded</u> our <u>fathers</u> that they should <u>teach</u> their children.

Now we get to exactly WHAT the psalmist means by "high sentences". So there is no mistake, He says it in two different ways. And then He re-states the mandate for us dads again. Couldn't be much simpler or clearer.

**Put It Together Using the Tide Technique**

2 I will open my <u>mouth</u> in a <u>parable</u>. I will <u>declare</u> the high <u>sentences</u> of old.
3 Which we have <u>heard</u> and <u>known</u>, and our <u>fathers</u> have <u>told</u> us.
4 We will not <u>hide</u> them from their <u>children</u>. But to the <u>generation</u> that is to come, we will show the <u>praise</u> of the Lord, His <u>power</u> also, and His <u>wonderful</u> <u>works</u> that He has done.
5 How He established a <u>testimony</u> in <u>Jacob</u>, and ordained a <u>Law</u> in <u>Israel</u>, which He <u>commanded</u> our <u>fathers</u> that they should <u>teach</u> their children.

Memo Devo
**Psalm 78:2-7**
**Subject: Family Discipleship**

**DAY 5**
**Psalm 78:6**

6 That the <u>posterity</u> might <u>know</u> it. And the <u>children</u> which should be born might <u>stand</u> up and <u>declare</u> it to their <u>children</u>.

In my opinion this is one of the most overt statements in the Bible about God's desire for us to memorize, speak back and ponder His Word together with our children. Notice that the actions in the second sentence are "stand up" and "declare". Those are not exactly passive verbs. I think this shows that God is not satisfied with the next generation only sitting and reading the Bible in churches, synagogues and at schools, but He desires it to be actively declared out loud at home, as it was done for the 2700 years between Adam and Moses.

**Put It Together Using the Tide Technique**

2 I will open my <u>mouth</u> in a <u>parable</u>. I will <u>declare</u> the high <u>sentences</u> of old.
3 Which we have <u>heard</u> and <u>known</u>, and our <u>fathers</u> have <u>told</u> us.
4 We will not <u>hide</u> them from their <u>children</u>. But to the <u>generation</u> that is to come, we will show the <u>praise</u> of the Lord, His <u>power</u> also, and His <u>wonderful</u> <u>works</u> that He has done.
5 How He established a <u>testimony</u> in <u>Jacob</u>, and ordained a <u>Law</u> in <u>Israel</u>, which He <u>commanded</u> our <u>fathers</u> that they should <u>teach</u> their children.
6 That the <u>posterity</u> might <u>know</u> it. And the <u>children</u> which should be born might <u>stand</u> up and <u>declare</u> it to their <u>children</u>.

Memo Devo
**Psalm 78:2-7**
**Subject: Family Discipleship**

**DAY 6**
**Psalm 78:7**

7 That they might set their <u>hope</u> on God, and not forget the <u>works</u> of God, but keep His <u>commandments</u>.

The ultimate goal of Scripture memorization with oral recitation or dramatization is to draw nearer to God, that we may love Him better. This is the promise Jesus repeats in John 14:15 ("If you love me, keep my commandments.") and John 17:17 ("Sanctify them by the Truth. Your Word is Truth.")

**Put It Together Using the Tide Technique**

2 I will open my <u>mouth</u> in a <u>parable</u>. I will <u>declare</u> the high <u>sentences</u> of old.
3 Which we have <u>heard</u> and <u>known</u>, and our <u>fathers</u> have <u>told</u> us.
4 We will not <u>hide</u> them from their <u>children</u>. But to the <u>generation</u> that is to come, we will show the <u>praise</u> of the Lord, His <u>power</u> also, and His <u>wonderful</u> <u>works</u> that He has done.
5 How He established a <u>testimony</u> in <u>Jacob</u>, and ordained a <u>Law</u> in <u>Israel</u>, which He <u>commanded</u> our <u>fathers</u> that they should <u>teach</u> their children.
6 That the <u>posterity</u> might <u>know</u> it. And the <u>children</u> which should be born might <u>stand</u> up and <u>declare</u> it to their <u>children</u>.
7 That they might set their <u>hope</u> on God, and not forget the <u>works</u> of God, but keep His <u>commandments</u>.

# "Love"
## 1Corinthians 13:1-10

Memo Devo
**1Corinthians 13:1-10**
**Subject: Love**

**DAY 1**
**1Corinthians 13:1**

1 If I speak in <u>languages</u> of men and of angels, but have not love, I am but sounding <u>brass</u> or a clanging <u>cymbal</u>.

This is the first of four examples given of things I can perform without reward if I am motivated by something other than God's love. So I really hone in on the word "language". Sounding brass and clanging cymbal are such fun images, quite frankly, that I don't have much trouble remembering them.

**Point to Ponder**

One thing I've noticed recently is how similar this passage is to the Beatitudes (Matt 5:3-16). Jesus' warning is the same in both passages. He is telling me that the true starting point of my love must be from a state of total desperation for His completing power (2Cor12:9). Ironically, the first step in loving like Jesus is realizing I have NO shot at doing so. (cf Matt 5:20, 48)

Memo Devo
**1Corinthians 13:1-10**
**Subject: Love**

**DAY 2**
**1Corinthians 13:2**

2 And if I have the gift of <u>Prophecy</u>, and know all <u>secrets</u> and all <u>knowledge</u>, and have all <u>faith</u>, so that I can move <u>mountains</u>, but have not love, I am <u>nothing</u>.

**Mnemonic: SKAF-folding**

The second of four examples given of things I can perform without reward if I am motivated by something other than God's love. This time, the Spiritual Gift of Prophecy takes center stage. Then it's just a matter of arranging those next descriptive keywords. I use a wacky acronym for the words "secrets", "knowledge", "all" and "faith" or S-K-A-F, then add "-folding" onto the end. This is logical in that it suggests climbing, as in a mountian (even though I risk offending the spelling police). The last phrase is tricky for me too because of its similarity to the last phrase in verse 3. However, the keywords at the end of each verse, "nothing" and "profit", are in alphabetical order. So that helps.

**\*Put It Together**

1 If I speak in <u>languages</u> of men and of angels, but have not love, I am but sounding <u>brass</u> or a clanging <u>cymbal</u>.
2 And if I have the gift of <u>Prophecy</u>, and know all <u>secrets</u> and all <u>knowledge</u>, and have all <u>faith</u>, so that I can move <u>mountains</u>, but have not love, I am <u>nothing</u>.

\*Remember, a good rule of thumb during this first short-term memorization stage is 10 repetitions. Have fun! Work Hard! #:-D

Memo Devo
**1Corinthians 13:1-10**
**Subject: Love**

**DAY 3**
**1Corinthians 13:3**

3 And if I <u>feed</u> the poor with all my <u>goods</u>, and if I <u>give</u> my <u>body</u> to be <u>broken</u>, but have not love, it <u>profits</u> me nothing.


**Mnemonic: "FiG"**

The third and fourth of four examples given of things I can perform without reward if I am motivated by something other than God's love. I use the acronym "FiG" for the words "feeding" and "give" (an easy word for believers to remember, right?) That seems to give my brain all it needs to remember all the other keywords and phrases in this one. And there's that last phrase, with the "p"-word "profits" coming alphabetically after the keyword "nothing" from verse 2.


**The Tide Technique**

In the interests of convenience, I'm gonna repeat the actual memorization technique that I use once again. If you already remember it well, feel free to skip on to the next devo. After having put verse 3 in my short-term memory, rather than going back to verse 1 and trying to run all three verses together just yet, I first only go back to verse 2 and begin there, running 2 and 3 until I can do just those without looking. Only then do I go back and add verse 1 and try to do the whole passage together, like a tide slowly going in and out over the whole passage.

# Memo Devo
## 1Corinthians 13:1-10
## Subject: Love

## DAY 4
## 1Corinthians 13:4

4 Love is <u>patient</u>. Love is <u>kind</u>. Love does <u>not</u> <u>envy</u>. Love does not <u>boast</u> and is not <u>puffed</u> up.


### Mnemonic: Pekingese

Pekingese?!?! WHAT!? Bear with me here. Pekingese is usually pronounced "Pekinese", right? That makes it a quirky, yet memorable way to express the acronym, "PKNE", which stands for the words "patient", "kind", "not" and "envy". Then the last two keywords are pretty much different forms of the same word so I usually get those down without too much effort.

### Put It Together Using the *Tide Technique

1 If I speak in <u>languages</u> of men and of angels, but have not love, I am but sounding <u>brass</u> or a clanging <u>cymbal</u>.
2 And if I have the gift of <u>Prophecy</u>, and know all <u>secrets</u> and all <u>knowledge</u>, and have all <u>faith</u>, so that I can move <u>mountains</u>, but have not love, I am <u>nothing</u>.
3 And if I <u>feed</u> the poor with all my <u>goods</u>, and if I <u>give</u> my <u>body</u> to be <u>broken</u>, but have not love, it <u>profits</u> me nothing.
4 Love is <u>patient</u>. Love is <u>kind</u>. Love does <u>not</u> envy. Love does not <u>boast</u> and is not <u>puffed</u> up.


*More information on the Tide Technique can be found elsewhere in this book and also on my instructional video "Bible Play: The Value of Dramatization in Memorization" available at 5talentsaudio.com.

Memo Devo
**1Corinthians 13:1-10**
**Subject: Love**

**DAY 5**
**1Corinthians 13:5**

5 It is not <u>rude</u>. It is not <u>selfish</u>. It is not <u>provoked</u> to <u>anger</u>. It <u>thinks</u> no <u>evil</u>.

**Mnemonic: "no Rude SPATs"**

This is one of my favorite mnemonic acronyms. It is such a logical application of the teaching, don't you think? I could also use "no Rude SPATEs" if I wanted to include all the keywords.

**Put It Together Using the *Tide Technique**

1 If I speak in <u>languages</u> of men and of angels, but have not love, I am but sounding <u>brass</u> or a clanging <u>cymbal</u>.
2 And if I have the gift of <u>Prophecy</u>, and know all <u>secrets</u> and all <u>knowledge</u>, and have all <u>faith</u>, so that I can move <u>mountains</u>, but have not love, I am <u>nothing</u>.
3 And if I <u>feed</u> the poor with all my <u>goods</u>, and if I <u>give</u> my <u>body</u> to be <u>broken</u>, but have not love, it <u>profits</u> me nothing.
4 Love is <u>patient</u>. Love is <u>kind</u>. Love does <u>not</u> <u>envy</u>. Love does not <u>boast</u> and is not <u>puffed</u> up.
5 It is not <u>rude</u>. It is not <u>selfish</u>. It is not <u>provoked</u> to <u>anger</u>. It <u>thinks</u> no <u>evil</u>.

*Remember, start at the end and "tide back", adding one verse at a time, anchoring each phrase to its keyword trigger or mnemonic.

Memo Devo
**1Corinthians 13:1-10**
**Subject: Love**

**DAY 6**
**1Corinthians 13:6**

6 It does not rejoice in injustice, but rejoices in the truth.

Obviously "rejoice" is the main keyword in verse 6. Then it's just about remembering the other two. Many translations use "unrighteousness" instead. I just happen to think "injustice" better conveys the Greek word here (adikia). Plus, I don't think this is only referring to unrighteous behavior in the modern religious sense.

**Put It Together Using the Tide Technique**

*...2 And if I have the gift of Prophecy, and know all secrets and all knowledge, and have all faith, so that I can move mountains, but have not love, I am nothing.
3 And if I feed the poor with all my goods, and if I give my body to be broken, but have not love, it profits me nothing.
4 Love is patient. Love is kind. Love does not envy. Love does not boast and is not puffed up.
5 It is not rude. It is not selfish. It is not provoked to anger. It thinks no evil.
6 It does not rejoice in injustice, but rejoices in the truth.

*Notice I've only put the last 5 verses up. This is to demonstrate what I mean about only reciting THIS WEEK'S verses every Friday. It's good to bite off sections at a time.

Memo Devo
**1Corinthians 13:1-10**
**Subject: Love**

**DAY 7**
**1Corinthians 13:7**

7 It <u>bears</u> all things. It <u>believes</u> all things. It <u>hopes</u> all things. It <u>endures</u> <u>all</u> <u>things</u>.

**Mnemonic: "BE HEAT"**

Another one of my favorite mnemonics. B-E H-E-A-T. An acronym for the two "b" words and then "hopes", "endures", "all" and "things". It not only implies being an oasis of warmth in an otherwise cold world, but it also conjurs the image of making someone a bit uncomfortable if need be. Not to mention just being "on fire" for the Lord, right?

**Put It Together Using the Tide Technique**

...3 And if I <u>feed</u> the poor with all my <u>goods</u>, and if I <u>give</u> my <u>body</u> to be <u>broken</u>, but have not love, it <u>profits</u> me nothing.
4 Love is <u>patient</u>. Love is <u>kind</u>. Love does <u>not</u> <u>envy</u>. Love does not <u>boast</u> and is not <u>puffed</u> up.
5 It is not <u>rude</u>. It is not <u>selfish</u>. It is not <u>provoked</u> to <u>anger</u>. It <u>thinks</u> no <u>evil</u>.
6 It does not <u>rejoice</u> in <u>injustice</u>, but rejoices in the <u>truth</u>.
7 It <u>bears</u> all things. It <u>believes</u> all things. It <u>hopes</u> all things. It <u>endures</u> <u>all</u> <u>things</u>.

Memo Devo
**1Corinthians 13:1-10**
**Subject: Love**

**DAY 8**
**1Corinthians 13:8**

8 Love never <u>fails,</u> even after <u>prophecies</u> are ended, <u>languages</u> cease and <u>knowledge</u> fades away.

No mnemonic for this one, but it's basically a restating of the first three verses. Tell 'em what you're gonna tell 'em. Tell 'em. And then tell 'em whatcha told em. Who knew Dale Carnegie was a disciple of St. Paul?!

**Put It Together Using the \*Tide Technique**

...4 Love is <u>patient</u>. Love is <u>kind</u>. Love does <u>not</u> <u>envy</u>. Love does not <u>boast</u> and is not <u>puffed</u> up.
5 It is not <u>rude</u>. It is not <u>selfish</u>. It is not <u>provoked</u> to <u>anger</u>. It <u>thinks</u> no <u>evil</u>.
6 It does not <u>rejoice</u> in <u>injustice</u>, but rejoices in the <u>truth</u>.
7 It <u>bears</u> all things. It <u>believes</u> all things. It <u>hopes</u> all things. It <u>endures</u> <u>all</u> <u>things</u>.
8 Love never <u>fails,</u> even after <u>prophecies</u> are ended, <u>languages</u> cease and <u>knowledge</u> fades away.

\*Remember, start at the end and "tide" back, phrase by phrase, anchoring to your keywords, until you reach the beginning. A good rule of thumb is 10 reps per verse, but don't move on until you can comfortably speak back at least the last 5 verses.

# Memo Devo
## 1Corinthians 13:1-10
## Subject: Love

**DAYS 9 & 10**
**1Corinthians 13:9-10**

9 For we know in part and we prophesy in part. 10 But when That which is perfect comes, then that which is in part shall be abolished.

I put these last two together since they are parts of the same thought, which is essentially a re-statement of Jesus' words from Matthew 5:17.

**Put It Together Using the Tide Technique**

1 If I speak in languages of men and of angels, but have not love, I am but sounding brass or a clanging cymbal.
2 And if I have the gift of Prophecy, and know all secrets and all knowledge, and have all faith, so that I can move mountains, but have not love, I am nothing.
3 And if I feed the poor with all my goods, and if I give my body to be broken, but have not love, it profits me nothing.
4 Love is patient. Love is kind. Love does not envy. Love does not boast and is not puffed up.
5 It is not rude. It is not selfish. It is not provoked to anger. It thinks no evil.
6 It does not rejoice in injustice, but rejoices in the truth.
7 It bears all things. It believes all things. It hopes all things. It endures all things.
8 Love never fails, even after prophecies are ended, languages cease and knowledge fades away.
9 For we know in part and we prophesy in part. 10 But when That which is perfect comes, then that which is in part shall be abolished.

# "The Beatitudes"
## Matthew 5:3-16

www.5talentsaudio.com

Memo Devo
**Matthew 5:3-16**
**Subject: The Beatitudes**

**DAY 1**
**Matthew 5:3**

3 Blessed are the <u>poor</u> in spirit, for theirs is the <u>kingdom</u> of heaven.

The reward Jesus gives here is the same as the one He gives in v10, nicely bookending these first 8 single-sentence blessings. That helps me remember both. Otherwise, as always, I underline the keywords first. This helps me group phrases together in my mind using a single word trigger, similar to a phenomenon known as "typoglycemia", whereby our brains are able to complete words even if we only have the first and last letters in the proper place. Tihs is bcuseae the huamn mnid deos not raed ervey lteter by istlef. And in my experience, the same thing applies to phrases. God seems to have designed our brains without a need for very much to go on when it comes to processing text.

**Point to Ponder**

The Beatitudes are conditions of the heart that are not just God's blessings on me, but more importantly my blessings on God. As I have memorized and pondered them, the Spirit has shown me how much they are related to 1Corinthians 13 in that they clearly state the kind of love that only He can provide, but nevertheless the kind of love that He expects from me. Hmmm. Seems I better be seeking help from somewhere. And that somewhere is Jesus!

Memo Devo
**Matthew 5:3-16**
**Subject: The Beatitudes**

**DAY 2**
**Matthew 5:4**

4 Blessed are those who mourn, for they shall be comforted.

**Mnemonic: "PM"**

The main keyword in 7 out of the first 8 Beatitudes begins with either a 'p' or an 'm'; poor, mourn, meek (skip v6 which is hunger, although us mnemonic geeks might easily substitute pangs or munchies I suppose) then merciful, pure, peacemakers and persecuted. For me, that's very helpful in remembering them.

**\*Put It Together**

3 Blessed are the poor in spirit, for theirs is the kingdom of heaven.
4 Blessed are those who mourn, for they shall be comforted.

\*Again, about 10 repetitions per verse seems right for this first short-term memorization stage. After that, I try to recite each verse, each day, for someone else, with a cumulative recitation of all the verses on Friday or the weekend. But if no one else is around, another way to check if something is getting into my long-term memory is to speak the verse back out loud to myself while juggling or folding laundry or doing some other simple task that creates a mild distraction for my brain. Try it!

Memo Devo
**Matthew 5:3-16**
**Subject: The Beatitudes**

**DAY 3**
**Matthew 5:5**

5 Blessed are the <u>meek</u>, for they shall <u>inherit</u> the earth.


**Mnemonic: "PM"**

Meek is a similar word to 'charity' in that it's an old-fashioned way to say a slightly broader-meaning modern word. The modern form of 'charity' is 'love' and the modern form of 'meek' is 'humble' (or 'praios' if you're following along in Greek.) Humility is such a blessing to God. It's how Jesus describes Himself in Matt 11:29 and it's one of the Fruits given by His Spirit in Galatians 5:22-23.


**The *Tide Technique**

3 Blessed are the <u>poor</u> in spirit, for theirs is the <u>kingdom</u> of heaven.
4 Blessed are those who <u>mourn</u>, for they shall be <u>comforted</u>.
5 Blessed are the <u>meek</u>, for they shall <u>inherit</u> the earth.


*So simple yet so effective! After having put verse 5 in my short-term memory, rather than going back to verse 3 and trying to run all three verses that I have learned together just yet, I first only go back to verse 4 and begin there, running 4 and 5 until I can do just those two comfortably. Only then do I go back and add verse 3, like a tide slowly going in and out over the whole passage. My brain feels less stressed and is more encouraged by more successful run-throughs of smaller sections. And success and confidence breeds more success and confidence!

Memo Devo
**Matthew 5:3-16**
**Subject: The Beatitudes**

**DAY 4**
**Matthew 5:6**

6 Blessed are those who <u>hunger</u> and thirst for righteousness, for they shall be <u>filled</u>.

Another beautifully poetic variation on Matt 5:3 and all the Beatitudes really. The point is to humbly focus my heart on Him, and trust Him to take care of the rest. Jesus echoes this same specific thing again later in the Sermon on the Mount, interestingly enough within the context of hungering and thirsting to have all the answers myself. (Matt 6:33)

Have fun. Be humble. #:-D

**Put It Together Using the *Tide Technique**

3 Blessed are the <u>poor</u> in spirit, for theirs is the <u>kingdom</u> of heaven.
4 Blessed are those who <u>mourn</u>, for they shall be <u>comforted</u>.
5 Blessed are the <u>meek</u>, for they shall <u>inherit</u> the earth.
6 Blessed are those who <u>hunger</u> and thirst for righteousness, for they shall be <u>filled</u>.

*Don't forget to speak the verses back to someone else once you think you have a pretty good handle on them. Or at the very least, recite them to yourself while doing a simple task such as juggling or yard work or folding laundry, etc.

Memo Devo
**Matthew 5:3-16**
**Subject: The Beatitudes**

**DAY 5**
**Matthew 5:7**

7 Blessed are the <u>merciful</u>, for they shall receive <u>mercy</u>.

**Mnemonic: "PM"**

Again, every keyword for these first 8 Beatitudes does or could, at least, start with either a 'p' or an 'm'. And this one is extra easy because they are basically the same word.

**Put It Together Using the *Tide Technique**

3 Blessed are the <u>poor</u> in spirit, for theirs is the <u>kingdom</u> of heaven.
4 Blessed are those who <u>mourn</u>, for they shall be <u>comforted</u>.
5 Blessed are the <u>meek</u>, for they shall <u>inherit</u> the earth.
6 Blessed are those who <u>hunger</u> and thirst for righteousness, for they shall be <u>filled</u>.
7 Blessed are the <u>merciful</u>, for they shall receive <u>mercy</u>.


*If you have kids like me, there are a couple of ways I've found to include them in my recitations each morning. The first is simply to pray the words that I've memorized over breakfast. And the second way is a little game we call "Wrong O Daddy O!", because that's what they yell if I mess up my recitation for them. They actually get out their Bibles (or this book), follow along, and give me the old buzzer-oo if I change so much as a jot or a tittle. It's a lot of fun for them, but at the same time it shows them my love for Jesus in a small way every day, while giving me the accountability I need for successful long-term memorization.

# Memo Devo
**Matthew 5:3-16**
**Subject: The Beatitudes**

## DAY 6
**Matthew 5:8**

8 Blessed are the <u>pure</u> in heart, for they shall <u>see</u> God.

## Mnemonic: "PM"

Again, every keyword for these first 8 Beatitudes does or could, at least, start with either a 'p' or an 'm'.

## Point to Ponder

For this one, cross-referencing Matt 5:48 and 1Cor 13:9-10 really helps me with the logic of it and thus helps me memorize it. I cannot ever be truly pure in heart (i.e. perfect) in this life. And if I were to remain in this state, the reality is that I can never be with God in the next life. But by the grace of a loving God, I can do BOTH if I truly repent of my sin and believe in the pure and perfect atoning blood sacrifice of Jesus Christ on the Cross. That's it! It truly is amazing, isn't it?

## Put It Together Using the Tide Technique

...4 Blessed are those who <u>mourn</u>, for they shall be <u>comforted</u>.
5 Blessed are the <u>meek</u>, for they shall <u>inherit</u> the earth.
6 Blessed are those who <u>hunger</u> and thirst for righteousness, for they shall be <u>filled</u>.
7 Blessed are the <u>merciful</u>, for they shall receive <u>mercy</u>.
8 Blessed are the <u>pure</u> in heart, for they shall <u>see</u> God.

Memo Devo
**Matthew 5:3-16**
**Subject: The Beatitudes**

**DAY 7**
**Matthew 5:9**

9 Blessed are the <u>peacemakers</u>, for they shall be called the <u>children</u> of God.

**Mnemonic: "PM"**

Again, every keyword for these first 8 Beatitudes does or could, at least, start with either a 'p' or an 'm'.

**Point to Ponder**

Peacemakers are not just people who break up fights, they are primarily those who emulate Jesus by bringing His peace to the tired, hopeless and downtrodden. Just as the heavenly soldiers proclaimed when He was born, "Peace in earth. And toward men, goodwill." (Luke 2:14) And just as He himself proclaimed just before He died, "I have told you these things so that in Me you may have peace." (John 16:33)

**Put It Together Using the Tide Technique**

...5 Blessed are the <u>meek</u>, for they shall <u>inherit</u> the earth.
6 Blessed are those who <u>hunger</u> and thirst for righteousness, for they shall be <u>filled</u>.
7 Blessed are the <u>merciful</u>, for they shall receive <u>mercy</u>.
8 Blessed are the <u>pure</u> in heart, for they shall <u>see</u> God.
9 Blessed are the <u>peacemakers</u>, for they shall be called the <u>children</u> of God.

Memo Devo
**Matthew 5:3-16**
**Subject: The Beatitudes**

**DAY 8**
**Matthew 5:10**

10 Blessed are those who are <u>persecuted</u> for righteousness' sake, for theirs is the <u>kingdom</u> of heaven.

**Mnemonic: "PM"**

In addition to being the final 'p' keyword to the puzzle that is the first 8 Beatitudes, this verse also contains the other "bookend" of the same exact reward I find in verse 3, the "kingdom of heaven". Hey, anything and everything can be a memory aid!

**Put It Together Using the *Tide Technique**

...6 Blessed are those who <u>hunger</u> and thirst for righteousness, for they shall be <u>filled</u>.
7 Blessed are the <u>merciful</u>, for they shall receive <u>mercy</u>.
8 Blessed are the <u>pure</u> in heart, for they shall <u>see</u> God.
9 Blessed are the <u>peacemakers</u>, for they shall be called the <u>children</u> of God.
10 Blessed are those who are <u>persecuted</u> for righteousness' sake, for theirs is the <u>kingdom</u> of heaven.

*Remember, start at the end and "tide back", adding one verse at a time, anchoring each phrase to its keyword trigger or mnemonic. Then on Friday or over the weekend, try to speak back the last five verses to someone. You can do this! #:-D

Memo Devo
**Matthew 5:3-16**
**Subject: The Beatitudes**

**DAY 9**
**Matthew 5:11**

11 Blessed are you when others <u>revile</u> you, and <u>people</u> <u>utter</u> all <u>kinds</u> of <u>evil</u> against you <u>falsely</u> for My sake.


**Mnemonic: "PUKE"**

Forgive the crudeness, but this mnemonic really is perfect for this verse. Especially when I ponder what must have transpired on the way out of Jerusalem up to Golgotha. Blessed are you when people p_ _ _ on you for My sake.

**P**eople **U**tter all **K**inds of **E**vil...


**Put It Together Using the *Tide Technique**

...7 Blessed are the <u>merciful</u>, for they shall receive <u>mercy</u>.
8 Blessed are the <u>pure</u> in heart, for they shall <u>see</u> God.
9 Blessed are the <u>peacemakers</u>, for they shall be called the <u>children</u> of God.
10 Blessed are those who are <u>persecuted</u> for righteousness' sake, for theirs is the <u>kingdom</u> of heaven.
11 Blessed are you when others <u>revile</u> you, and <u>people</u> <u>utter</u> all <u>kinds</u> of <u>evil</u> against you <u>falsely</u> for My sake.


*More information on the Tide Technique can be found elsewhere in this book and also online at 5talentsaudio.com.

Memo Devo
**Matthew 5:3-16**
**Subject: The Beatitudes**

**DAY 10**
**Matthew 5:12**

12 Rejoice and be glad! Your reward is great in heaven! For so they persecuted the prophets who were before you.

This is the second half of the last "blessing" listed and completes verse 11. It's the only Beatitude to use the second person pronoun "you" rather than a general plural grouping. Not yet sure if that's significant theologically or not, but it definitely helps me remember it for some reason.

**Put It Together Using the Tide Technique**

...8 Blessed are the pure in heart, for they shall see God.
9 Blessed are the peacemakers, for they shall be called the children of God.
10 Blessed are those who are persecuted for righteousness' sake, for theirs is the kingdom of heaven.
11 Blessed are you when others revile you, and people utter all kinds of evil against you falsely for My sake.
12 Rejoice and be glad! Your reward is great in heaven! For so they persecuted the prophets who were before you.

Memo Devo
**Matthew 5:3-16**
**Subject: The Beatitudes**

**DAY 11**
**Matthew 5:13**

13 You are the <u>salt</u> of the earth. But if salt <u>loses</u> its saltiness, how can it be <u>made</u> salty again? It is <u>no longer good</u> for anything except to be <u>thrown</u> out and <u>trampled</u> underfoot.

Some don't include vv13-16 in the Beatitudes. I do because they reinforce the fact that these are as much OUR blessings on God as they are HIS blessings on us.

**Put It Together Using the *Tide Technique**

...9 Blessed are the <u>peacemakers</u>, for they shall be called the <u>children</u> of God.
10 Blessed are those who are <u>persecuted</u> for righteousness' sake, for theirs is the <u>kingdom</u> of heaven.
11 Blessed are you when others <u>revile</u> you, and <u>people utter</u> all <u>kinds</u> of <u>evil</u> against you <u>falsely</u> for My sake.
12 <u>Rejoice</u> and be glad! Your <u>reward</u> is great! For so they <u>persecuted</u> the <u>prophets</u> who were before you.
13 You are the <u>salt</u> of the earth. But is salt <u>loses</u> its saltiness, how can it be <u>made</u> salty again? It is <u>no longer good</u> for anything except to be <u>thrown</u> out and <u>trampled</u> underfoot.

*Tomorrow I'll add the final 3 verses, and begin what I suppose might be called the "High Tide" part of this technique. That is, the time when I begin to add my weekly 5-verse sections together, tiding my way back, bit by bit, to the beginning.

# Memo Devo
## Matthew 5:3-16
## Subject: The Beatitudes

**DAYS 12-14**
**Matthew 5:14-16**

14 You are the light of the world. A city set on a hill cannot be hidden. 15 Nor does anyone light a lamp and put it under a basket, but on a stand. And it gives light to all who are in the house. 16 So likewise, let your light shine before others that they may see your good works and give glory to your Father Who is in heaven.

These famous verses are most memorable to me when I put them in their complete context.

## Put It Together Using the Tide Technique

3 Blessed are the poor in spirit, for theirs is the kingdom of heaven.
4 Blessed are those who mourn, for they shall be comforted.
5 Blessed are the meek, for they shall inherit the earth.
6 Blessed are those who hunger and thirst for righteousness, for they shall be filled.
7 Blessed are the merciful, for they shall receive mercy.
8 Blessed are the pure in heart, for they shall see God.
9 Blessed are the peacemakers, for they shall be called the children of God.
10 Blessed are those who are persecuted for righteousness' sake, for theirs is the kingdom of heaven.
11 Blessed are you when others revile you, and people utter all kinds of evil against you falsely for My sake.
12 Rejoice and be glad! Your reward is great! For so they persecuted the prophets who were before you.
13 You are the salt of the earth. But is salt loses its saltiness, how can it be made salty again? It is no longer good for anything except to be thrown out and trampled underfoot.
14 You are the light of the world. A city set on a hill cannot be hidden. 15 Nor does anyone light a lamp and put it under a basket, but on a stand. And it gives light to all who are in the house. 16 So likewise, let your light shine before others that they may see your good works and give glory to your Father Who is in heaven.

# "Jesus' Deity, Our Adoption"
## John 1:1-18

Memo Devo
**John 1:1-18**
**Subject: Jesus' Deity, Our Adoption (as Christians)**

**DAY 1**
**John 1:1**

1 In the <u>beginning</u> was the <u>Word</u>. And the Word was <u>with</u> God. And the Word <u>was</u> God.

This verse is like many famous verses in that it holds both powerful truth and deep controversy at the same time. However, this is only the first of several times within this passage that John explicitly names Jesus as God. And he does it in many different ways, as if anticipating the question and wanting to make sure there is no mistake.
I have underlined the keywords even though I have no mnemonic in place. Again, this helps me group phrases together in my mind using a single keyword trigger. Bcuseae the huamn mnid deos not raed ervey lteter by istlef. Nor does it read, at least in my experience, every word by itself either.

**Speak it Back**

I can't stress enough how important it is during this first short-term memorization stage to recite each verse out loud to someone else. But again, if I can't do that, I will speak the verse back to myself while I'm doing some mildly taxing activity like juggling, folding laundry or other simple task that creates a mild distraction for my brain. I also found out this is a common technique used by law students when studying for the bar. Go figure! Take your time and don't get discouraged. You can do this! Remember, people just like you did it for thousands of years before baby Moses was ever put in that basket. #:-D

Memo Devo
John 1:1-18
Subject: Jesus' Deity, Our Adoption (as Christians)

**DAY 2**
**John 1:2**

2 The <u>same</u> was in the beginning <u>with</u> God.

This is John's first re-statement of Jesus' deity. It's also a great proof text for part of the doctrine of the Trinity: that is, that there exists only One God, but as three distinct Persons; Father, Son and Holy Spirit.

I can see where this verse can be both clarifying and confusing at the same time. It's clarifying because it's saying that Jesus is not a created being. But perhaps it's confusing because it does not explicitly say He IS God like it just did in the previous verse.

But think about it logically. If I believe in One God, as the Bible clearly teaches in Deut. 6:4, Isaiah 44:6 and elsewhere. And I believe there are only two options for origin, eternal or created. Then Jesus must eternally exist, not as a separate god, but as a separate part of One God. I know, I get a headache thinking about it too quite frankly, but it turns out that's exactly what Jesus says in His Word. There is One God (Mark 12:29) and He is His eternal Son, sent to save us. (Mark 14:62)

**Put It Together Using the *Tide Technique**

1 In the <u>beginning</u> was the <u>Word</u>. And the Word was <u>with</u> God. And the Word <u>was</u> God.
2 The <u>same</u> was in the beginning <u>with</u> God.

Memo Devo
**John 1:1-18**
**Subject: Jesus' Deity, Our Adoption (as Christians)**

**DAY 3**
**John 1:3**

3 All things were <u>made</u> by Him. And <u>without</u> Him was <u>not</u> <u>anything</u> made that was made.

**Mnemonic: "Made Mammaw mad"**

John will stop at nothing to make his point about Jesus' deity. Here he even uses (gasp!) bad grammar! While my Mammaw must have grappled mightily with the double negative of "not anything" being made "without Him" (hence the mnemonic) I for one am comforted by John's obvious mission to persuade me first and foremost that Jesus was indeed Who He said He was: The Messiah (Mark 14:62)

**Put It Together Using the *Tide Technique**

1 In the <u>beginning</u> was the <u>Word</u>. And the Word was <u>with</u> God. And the Word <u>was</u> God.
2 The <u>same</u> was in the beginning with God.
3 All things were <u>made</u> by Him. And <u>without</u> Him was <u>not</u> <u>anything</u> made that was made.

*More information on the Tide Technique can be found elsewhere in this book and also on my instructional video "Bible Play: The Value of Dramatization in Memorization" available at 5talentsaudio.com.

# Memo Devo
**John 1:1-18**
**Subject: Jesus' Deity, Our Adoption (as Christians)**

**DAY 4**
**John 1:4**

4 In Him was life. And the life was the light of all people.

The common version of this verse uses the noun 'men' at the end. But when I looked it up in the Greek, the word is 'anthropos', which means 'man-faced' or 'humans'. On the other hand, the Greek word for 'men' is 'andres'. While I am usually very reluctant to "modernize" gender words in the Bible, I do agree with the practice when it is clearly applicable and this seems to be one of those places.

## Put It Together Using the Tide Technique

1 In the beginning was the Word. And the Word was with God. And the Word was God.
2 The same was in the beginning with God.
3 All things were made by Him. And without Him was not anything made that was made.
4 In Him was life. And the life was the light of all people.

## Wrong O Daddy O! (WODO)

I love to recite for my kids every morning at breakfast. One way I do this is with a game we call "Wrong O Daddy O!" because that's what they say if I mess up. It's a lot of fun for them, but at the same time it shows them my love for Jesus in a small way every day, while giving me the accountability I need for successful long-term memorization. If you're worried about getting food on your Bible, you have my permission to use this book instead. #;-D

Memo Devo
**John 1:1-18**
**Subject: Jesus' Deity, Our Adoption (as Christians)**

**DAY 5**
**John 1:5**

5 And the light <u>shines</u> in the darkness. And the <u>darkness</u> has not <u>understood</u> it.

A poetic statement of Jesus' whole ministry on this earth really, at once echoing Genesis 1:3 and foreshadowing John 8:12.

**Put It Together Using the Tide Technique**

1 In the <u>beginning</u> was the <u>Word</u>. And the Word was <u>with</u> God. And the Word <u>was</u> God.
2 The <u>same</u> was in the beginning with God.
3 All things were <u>made</u> by Him. And <u>without</u> Him was <u>not</u> <u>anything</u> made that was made.
4 In Him was <u>life</u>. And the life was the <u>light</u> of all people.
5 And the light <u>shines</u> in the darkness. And the <u>darkness</u> has not <u>understood</u> it.

# Memo Devo
## John 1:1-18
## Subject: Jesus' Deity, Our Adoption (as Christians)

**DAY 6**
**John 1:6**

6 There was a man <u>sent</u> from God whose name was <u>John</u>.

I don't normally do devotionals on the weekends, except perhaps to catch up on some recitations, so the change of subject to John Baptist works out nicely as a kick-off to week #2 for me. As always, I try to use as few keywords as possible and my brain fills in the blanks from there.

**Point to Ponder**

This verse also reveals how important the Apostle John thinks John Baptist's testimony is to Jesus' identity as the Messiah. Remember, John Baptist believed in Jesus without ever seeing Him perform a single miracle. Not one. All he had to go on was a lingering Dove on His shoulder as confirmation. But he believed. (John 1:29)

**Put It Together Using the Tide Technique**

...2 The <u>same</u> was in the beginning with God.
3 All things were <u>made</u> by Him. And <u>without</u> Him was <u>not</u> <u>anything</u> made that was made.
4 In Him was <u>life</u>. And the life was the <u>light</u> of all people.
5 And the light <u>shines</u> in the darkness. And the <u>darkness</u> has not <u>understood</u> it.
6 There was a man <u>sent</u> from God whose name was <u>John</u>.

Memo Devo
**John 1:1-18**
**Subject: Jesus' Deity, Our Adoption (as Christians)**

**DAYS 7-9**
**John 1:7-9**

7 He came to <u>testify</u> and bear <u>witness</u> about the <u>Light</u>, so that <u>through</u> him all might <u>believe.</u>
8 He was <u>not</u> the Light, but came to bear witness <u>about</u> the Light.
9 That is, the <u>true</u> Light Who lights every <u>person</u> that <u>comes</u> into the world.

Since vv7-9 are basically three parts of the same thought, I group them together and budget three days to complete them. This provides me with a couple of "catch up" days if I've fallen behind a little.

For groups of verses like these, I might also employ a "rip tide" technique. I start with v7 and reverse the "tide" to go forward slowly instead of backward, still one sentence at a time, until I have all three verses safely tucked away in my short-term memory.

**Put It Together Using the Tide Technique**

...5 And the light <u>shines</u> in the darkness. And the <u>darkness</u> has not <u>understood</u> it.
6 There was a man <u>sent</u> from God whose name was <u>John</u>.
7 He came to <u>testify</u> and bear <u>witness</u> about the <u>Light</u>, so that <u>through</u> him all might <u>believe.</u>
8 He was <u>not</u> the Light, but came to bear witness <u>about</u> the Light.
9 That is, the <u>true</u> Light Who lights every <u>person</u> that <u>comes</u> into the world.

# Memo Devo
**John 1:1-18**
**Subject: Jesus' Deity, Our Adoption (as Christians)**

**DAY 10**
**John 1:10**

10 He was <u>in</u> the <u>world</u>. And the world was <u>made</u> by Him. And the world <u>knew</u> Him <u>not</u>.

**Mnemonic: "I aM oK"**

This is the third explicit statement of Jesus' deity in this passage (the fourth if you count v3 as two statements). It is obviously centered on the keyword 'world'. So I just associate that word with the three other keywords: 'in', 'made' and 'knew' (IMK or "I aM oK").

**Put It Together Using the *Tide Technique**

...6 There was a man <u>sent</u> from God whose name was <u>John</u>.
7 He came to <u>testify</u> and bear <u>witness</u> about the <u>Light</u>, so that <u>through</u> him all might <u>believe.</u>
8 He was <u>not</u> the Light, but came to bear witness <u>about</u> the Light.
9 That is, the <u>true</u> Light Who lights every <u>person</u> that <u>comes</u> into the world.
10 He was <u>in</u> the <u>world</u>. And the world was <u>made</u> by Him. And the world <u>knew</u> Him <u>not</u>.


*Notice I've only been putting up the last 5 verses each day. This is to demonstrate what I mean about only reciting THIS WEEK'S verses every Friday. It's good to bite off small sections at a time. Next week I'll begin to make my way back to the beginning. But for now, I just think in terms of what I've added this week.

Memo Devo
**John 1:1-18**
**Subject: Jesus' Deity, Our Adoption (as Christians)**

**DAY 11-13**
**John 1:11-13**

11 He came to His <u>own</u> and His own <u>received</u> Him <u>not</u>. 12 <u>But</u> to as many as did <u>receive</u> Him, He gave the <u>right</u> to become <u>children</u> of God; that is, to those who <u>believe</u> in His <u>Name</u>, 13 who are <u>born</u>, not of <u>blood</u>, nor of the <u>will</u> of the <u>flesh</u>, nor of the will of <u>man</u>, but of <u>God</u>.

I know there's a lot here but it really is easier for me if I group these large single ideas into one. IMHO, this is one of the most beautiful and joyous statements in the whole Bible. It at once describes Jesus' unearned grace and unique power to save us and make us holy, through no effort of our own. Just by believing, we become siblings of the children of Israel, with full inheritance rights to the Kingdom. Oh my, what a glorious truth that is!

**Put It Together Using the *Tide Technique**

...8 He was <u>not</u> the Light, but came to bear witness <u>about</u> the Light. 9 That is, the <u>true</u> Light Who lights every <u>person</u> that <u>comes</u> into the world. 10 He was <u>in</u> the <u>world</u>. And the world was <u>made</u> by Him. And the world <u>knew</u> Him <u>not</u>.
11 He came to His <u>own</u> and His own <u>received</u> Him <u>not</u>. 12 <u>But</u> to as many as did <u>receive</u> Him, He gave the <u>right</u> to become <u>children</u> of God; that is, to those who <u>believe</u> in His <u>Name</u>, 13 who are <u>born</u>, not of <u>blood</u>, nor of the <u>will</u> of the <u>flesh</u>, nor of the will of <u>man</u>, but of <u>God</u>.

*an exception to the 5-verse rule because these six verses cover two complete thoughts.

Memo Devo
John 1:1-18
Subject: Jesus' Deity, Our Adoption (as Christians)

DAY 14
John 1:14

14 And the Word became flesh and dwelt among us. And we saw the glory thereof, as the glory of the Only begotten Son of the Father, full of grace and truth.

This famous verse is the fourth explicit statement of Jesus' deity in this passage.

**Put It Together Using the *Tide Technique**

...8 He was not the Light, but came to bear witness about the Light. 9 That is, the true Light Who lights every person that comes into the world. 10 He was in the world. And the world was made by Him. And the world knew Him not.
11 He came to His own and His own received Him not. 12 But to as many as did receive Him, He gave the right to become children of God; that is, to those who believe in His Name, 13 who are born, not of blood, nor of the will of the flesh, nor of the will of man, but of God.
14 And the Word became flesh and dwelt among us. And we saw the glory thereof, as the glory of the Only begotten Son of the Father, full of grace and truth.

*Start at the end and "tide" back, adding one phrase at a time and anchoring to the underlined keywords. Yours may be different, but I find that verbs and unusual words generally work best for me as keywords. Take your time. You can do this. Remember, memorization and dramatization was the only way us ordinary folks could study Scripture for almost HALF of our recorded existence (2700 years) before Moses began writing it all down.

# Memo Devo
**John 1:1-18**
**Subject: Jesus' Deity, Our Adoption (as Christians)**

**DAY 15**
**John 1:15**

15 John <u>bore</u> witness of Him, and <u>cried</u> out, saying, "This is He of whom I <u>spoke</u>! The <u>One</u> Who comes <u>after</u> me is <u>before</u> me. For He is <u>more</u> than me.

**Mnemonic: "Bore Before More"**

Rhymes are always conspicuous and fun and I like to take advantage of any that really work. Not sure about this one yet, quite frankly, but it's definitely worth a try. And I love the clever double entendre of the word 'before' that John uses.

**Put It Together Using the Tide Technique**

...11 He came to His <u>own</u> and His own <u>received</u> Him <u>not</u>. 12 <u>But</u> to as many as did <u>receive</u> Him, He gave the <u>right</u> to become <u>children</u> of God; that is, to those who <u>believe</u> in His <u>Name</u>, 13 who are <u>born</u>, not of <u>blood</u>, nor of the <u>will</u> of the <u>flesh</u>, nor of the will of <u>man</u>, but of <u>God</u>.
14 And the <u>Word</u> became <u>flesh</u> and dwelt among us. And we <u>saw</u> the glory thereof, as the <u>glory</u> of the <u>Only</u> begotten Son of the Father, full of <u>grace</u> and <u>truth</u>.
15 John <u>bore</u> witness of Him, and <u>cried</u> out, saying, "<u>This</u> is He of whom I <u>spoke</u>! The <u>One</u> Who comes <u>after</u> me Is <u>before</u> me. For He is <u>more</u> than me.

Memo Devo
**John 1:1-18**
**Subject: Jesus' Deity, Our Adoption (as Christians)**

**DAY 16**
**John 1:16**

16 And out of His <u>fullness</u> we have all received <u>grace</u> upon grace.

**Mnemonic: "Grace²"**

This one's very hard to translate at the end, but it seems to be saying the 'special' grace we receive from Jesus is over and above the 'common' grace we have already received from God.

**Put It Together Using the Tide Technique**

...11 He came to His <u>own</u> and His own <u>received</u> Him <u>not</u>. 12 <u>But</u> to as many as did <u>receive</u> Him, He gave the <u>right</u> to become <u>children</u> of God; that is, to those who <u>believe</u> in His <u>Name</u>, 13 who are <u>born</u>, not of <u>blood</u>, nor of the <u>will</u> of the <u>flesh</u>, nor of the will of <u>man</u>, but of <u>God</u>.
14 And the <u>Word</u> became <u>flesh</u> and dwelt among us. And we <u>saw</u> the glory thereof, as the <u>glory</u> of the <u>Only</u> begotten Son of the Father, full of <u>grace</u> and <u>truth</u>.
15 John <u>bore</u> witness of Him, and <u>cried</u> out, saying, "<u>This</u> is He of whom I <u>spoke</u>! The <u>One</u> Who comes <u>after</u> me Is <u>before</u> me. For He is <u>more</u> than me.
16 And out of His <u>fullness</u> we have all received <u>grace</u> upon grace.

# Memo Devo
**John 1:1-18**
**Subject: Jesus' Deity, Our Adoption (as Christians)**

**DAY 17**
**John 1:17**

17 For the <u>Law</u> was given by <u>Moses</u>, but <u>grace</u> and <u>truth</u> came by <u>Jesus</u> Christ.

This is a re-statement of Jesus' words recorded in another verse 17, Matthew 5:17.
I love verse symmetry!

**Put It Together Using the Tide Technique**

...11 He came to His <u>own</u> and His own <u>received</u> Him <u>not</u>. 12 <u>But</u> to as many as did <u>receive</u> Him, He gave the <u>right</u> to become <u>children</u> of God; that is, to those who <u>believe</u> in His <u>Name</u>, 13 who are <u>born</u>, not of <u>blood</u>, nor of the <u>will</u> of the <u>flesh</u>, nor of the will of <u>man</u>, but of <u>God</u>.
14 And the <u>Word</u> became <u>flesh</u> and dwelt among us. And we <u>saw</u> the glory thereof, as the <u>glory</u> of the <u>Only</u> begotten Son of the Father, full of <u>grace</u> and <u>truth</u>.
15 John <u>bore</u> witness of Him, and <u>cried</u> out, saying, "<u>This</u> is He of whom I <u>spoke</u>! The <u>One</u> Who comes <u>after</u> me Is <u>before</u> me. For He is <u>more</u> than me.
16 And out of His <u>fullness</u> we have all received <u>grace</u> upon grace.
17 For the <u>Law</u> was given by <u>Moses</u>, but <u>grace</u> and <u>truth</u> came by Jesus Christ.

# Memo Devo
## John 1:1-18
## Subject: Jesus' Deity, Our Adoption (as Christians)

**DAY 18**
**John 1:18**

18 No one has <u>seen</u> God. But the Only <u>Begotten</u> Son, Who is in the <u>bosom</u> of the Father, He has <u>declared</u> Him to us.

The final statement of Jesus' deity in this passage.

### Put It Together Using the Tide Technique

1 In the <u>beginning</u> was the <u>Word</u>. And the Word was <u>with</u> God. And the Word <u>was</u> God.
2 The <u>same</u> was in the beginning with God.
3 All things were <u>made</u> by Him. And <u>without</u> Him was <u>not anything</u> made that was made.
4 In Him was <u>life</u>. And the life was the <u>light</u> of all people.
5 And the light <u>shines</u> in the darkness. And the <u>darkness</u> has not <u>understood</u> it.
6 There was a man <u>sent</u> from God whose name was <u>John</u>.
7 He came to <u>testify</u> and bear <u>witness</u> about the <u>Light</u>, so that <u>through</u> him all might <u>believe.</u>
8 He was <u>not</u> the Light, but came to bear witness <u>about</u> the Light. 9 That is, the <u>true</u> Light Who lights every <u>person</u> that <u>comes</u> into the world. 10 He was <u>in</u> the <u>world</u>. And the world was <u>made</u> by Him. And the world <u>knew</u> Him <u>not</u>.
11 He came to His <u>own</u> and His own <u>received</u> Him <u>not</u>. 12 <u>But</u> to as many as did <u>receive</u> Him, He gave the <u>right</u> to become <u>children</u> of God; that is, to those who <u>believe</u> in His <u>Name</u>, 13 who are <u>born</u>, not of <u>blood</u>, nor of the will of the <u>flesh</u>, nor of the will of <u>man</u>, but of <u>God</u>.
14 And the <u>Word</u> became <u>flesh</u> and dwelt among us. And we <u>saw</u> the glory thereof, as the <u>glory</u> of the <u>Only</u> begotten Son of the Father, full of <u>grace</u> and <u>truth</u>.
15 John <u>bore</u> witness of Him, and <u>cried</u> out, saying, "<u>This</u> is He of whom I spoke! The <u>One</u> Who comes <u>after</u> me Is <u>before</u> me. For He is <u>more</u> than me.
16 And out of His <u>fullness</u> we have all received <u>grace</u> upon grace.
17 For the <u>Law</u> was given by <u>Moses</u>, but <u>grace</u> and <u>truth</u> came by Jesus Christ.
18 No one has <u>seen</u> God. But the Only <u>Begotten</u> Son, Who is in the <u>bosom</u> of the Father, He has <u>declared</u> Him to us.

"So shall my Word be that goes out of my mouth. It shall not return to me void. But it shall accomplish that which I will. And it shall prosper in the thing whereto I sent it."
Isaiah 55:11

www.5talentsaudio.com

Made in the USA
Charleston, SC
22 April 2014